The Memories I Keep

David Ritter

C000162863

Contact information:
david_ritter67@yahoo.com
Rittersrhymeandreason.org

THE MEMORIES I KEEP
Second Edition
Copyright © 2012 by David Ritter

ISBN-13: 979-8669515607

Contents

Dedication

This book is dedicated to my mother, Sandy Ritter. Mom is the one person in my life who has always been there for me, even during troubled times. When it comes to my writing, she has always been my biggest fan.

I love you, Mom!

Introduction

Many of my poems and short stories chronicle a lifelong struggle with the ups and downs of everyday life. They are direct, full of a variety of emotions, and usually have a message or meaning of social significance that most common folk can relate to. Rather than using complex imagery with flowery words, metaphors, and similes that most people don't understand, I try to keep it simple. Some poems have a personal meaning, others are only an idea, and some emerged from activities or challenges from a variety of writing avenues. Most of my poems rhyme because I like the challenge and they are, for me, simply more fun. These writing's, quite frankly, describe one man's beliefs and feelings about a world that is sometimes cruel. If "The Memories I Keep" can help someone smile, even if it's for a moment, then this world is a better place for us all and for that I feel good.

"I can do all things through Christ which strengtheneth me."
Philippians 4:13 KJV

Chapter 1:
FAMILIES ARE A
BLESSING

This Fathers Pride and Joy

There are few things in this world
that this Dad would truly treasure
more than what my bright son has done,
for he has brought me great pleasure.

He did not hit a long home run
nor throw a winning touchdown pass.
He did not bag a trophy buck
or reel in the state record bass.

Never voted homecoming king,
never dated the prom queen.
He did not get the play's lead
or enlist to be a Marine.

Now all of these things are noble
and would make any father proud.
But what my young man accomplished,
for me stands out above the crowd.

What is this fine deed my lad attained
that has brought this swelled Dad much joy?
He made the school's honor roll
so with pride I cheer," That's my boy!"

A Special Gift

Sixteen years ago today
God smiled down on me
Then handed me a special gift
For all the world to see

It changed my life forever
This treasure from above
And when I first saw it
I knew I was in love

It filled my heart with joy
Down inside my chest
I knew without a doubt
I was truly blessed

I held this special gift
My eyes filled with tears
And to this day I'm still humbled
Despite the passing years

This gift remains priceless
More precious than a pearl
And I will always cherish
My special baby girl

Parenthood

One thing remains in life that's good
The reward that comes with parenthood
Challenges and sorrow will fill some days
But triumph and joy will lead the way

Doctor visits and trips to the beach
ABCs and manners to teach
Writing out a Christmas list
Healing boo-boos with a kiss

Misplaced tools and spilled perfume
Countless dashes to the bathroom
Cleaning messes trippin' on toys
Birthday parties filled with noise

Smelly diapers and sleepless nights
Building a snowman and flying kites
School activities and learning to drive
Praying fervently they come back alive

Becoming a hero for smashing a bug
Mending a broken heart with just a hug
Rockin' a little one while they weep
A gentle song to aid their sleep

A baby's first steps and first word
The most pleasing sounds ears have heard
Until they grow with much to do
And reward you with an "I love you"

Challenges and sorrow will fill some days
But triumph and joy will lead the way
One thing remains in life that's good
The reward that comes with parenthood

Daddy's Prayers

Dear Precious Child,

Let your Daddy's prayers guide you
Down the path you choose to trod
So when you reach your journey's end
You will be face to face with God

And may He look down upon you
With a forever pleasing smile
'Cause Daddy's prayers alerted Him
Your each step to every mile

No need to ever worry
How or where the course may lead
If Daddy's not near to help you
Surely God will provide each need

In times when Daddy can't be near
Loneliness may invade your heart
Let your Daddy's prayers guide you
So we may never be apart

Always in my prayers,
Love, Daddy

My Precious Daughter

Here I lay all alone
thinking about how you've grown
You're getting big, you're almost two
I'll never forget the first time I held you

There's a big empty feeling in my heart
because we are so far apart
It was so hard to say goodbye
remembering curls and big brown eyes

Lately I've been feeling really sad
that you'll forget who is your dad
But I'll never forget my little girl
the greatest thing in this big world

If I had one wish, know what it would be?
For you to move and live with me
It's only what any dad would say
but I know your mom would say, "No way"

If there was a way Mom and I could share
I would show you how much I care
I'm sorry I left, it wasn't what I planned
someday I hope you'll understand

I've never missed someone this much, never
You'll be in my heart forever and ever
I'll come back, I just don't know when
I'll just keep missing you 'til then

I'm starting to cry like running water
I love and miss my precious daughter

The Christmas Ornament

Many years ago, when I was in kindergarten, I made a Christmas ornament to take home to my mother as a gift. This ornament was round and about the size of an orange. It was made of ceramic, white in color and very breakable, as our teacher continued to warn us. It was quite heavy, causing any branch that it would hang from to certainly bend under its burden. In the center of this cumbersome ornament was a picture molded of a log cabin set in a forest of pinecone trees. Snow capped mountains adorned the skyline behind the log cabin, to complete a beautiful winter scene.

It was my job to paint this scenic view, and paint it I did, with such tedious care. I was careful not to get any green paint from the tops of the pinecone trees on the snow-capped mountains, or any red paint, which I chose to paint the log cabin, on any of the pinecone trees. When I was done with this task, I stared at my prized gift in my little hands. In my eyes it was the most beautiful Christmas ornament in the whole class and I looked forward to giving it to my mother. I waited patiently for the sound of the bell indicating the end of another school day and the beginning of Christmas vacation. At the sound of that bell, I rushed out the door and swiftly ran home, careful not to drop my precious ornament, which I held clasped in my hands.

Upon entering the comforts of a warm home, I found Mom in the kitchen doing one of the many things a loving caring mother does while spending most of her day in the confines of that one room: She was cooking. Proudly, I looked up at her with my hands wrapped around my back. Suddenly, I reached out my hand to display the cherished gift that I had worked so carefully on and cried, "Merry Christmas!"

With a shriek of excitement, she dropped what she was doing, took the gift from my hands, and held it close to her heart.

"Is this for me?" she asked.

"Yes, I made it at school," I proudly explained.

"It is just beautiful," she declared, as she marched into the living room with me in tow.

Once inside the living room we stood before a tall Christmas tree that was full of colorful ornaments of all shapes and sizes. The tree also had a string of lights of different colors, some of which even blinked liked stars. Garland circled the tree several times from top to bottom and shimmering, silver tinsel was scattered all over the tree, which made the whole tree appear as if it was sparkling. It was topped with a star of different colored lights. To me, it was the most glamorous thing in the whole house, if not the whole world. While gazing upon this magnificent tree, mother proudly hung the ornament on a sturdy limb in the center of the tree, careful not to let it slip and fall on the bare hardwood floors below, where it would certainly break.

"I'm going to hang it right in the front so everyone can see it," she announced.

That's where it hung, year after year. With each approaching Christmas when it was time to venture into the attic to drag out our prized Christmas decorations, upon coming across this one particular ornament, she would always hold it up for the rest of the family to see, saying, "Look what David made in kindergarten." I would sheepishly look away, embarrassed by the childhood paint job of the bulky ornament and at the "aws" that would follow whenever Mom showed the ornament to family and friends.

As I grew older, I lost some interest in the things of Christmas, especially that ugly ornament. I didn't understand why Mom made such a fuss over something I had made when I was a small boy.

One Christmas season, when I was well into my teens, Mom painstakingly was gathering together all the Christmas decorations for yet another Christmas. She slowly walked up to me and with much sadness, held out her hands. There was the Christmas ornament, broken into what seemed like a million pieces.

"I accidentally dropped it," she frowned.
Being in a hurry to leave the house, I glanced at it and said, "It's okay, Mom."

"But you made it in kindergarten," she solemnly replied.

Not taking into consideration her feelings of sadness and regret, I grabbed my coat and said, "It's no big deal Mom, it was an ugly ornament anyway," as I quickly exited the house.

The next day, after spending the night with a friend, I came home to the sounds of glorious Christmas music echoing throughout the house.

Mom waited patiently for me to take off my winter gear, then walked up to me with her hands wrapped around her back.

"Guess what I got?" she said smiling.

"I don't know, what?"

She reached out her hand and in it was the ornament that had been broken into a million pieces. It had been glued back together. I said, "Wow, that doesn't look too bad," as I took it from her hand to further examine it. Realizing now how much that Christmas ornament meant to her, I hugged her and told her that I loved her. I then walked over and proudly hung the mended ornament on a sturdy limb in the center of the tree.

Looking back, I often wonder how long it must have taken my mom to glue that Christmas ornament back together. I really never expected to see the ornament again; yet, with her love, she took the time to put it back together for me.

To this day she continues to put things back together for me. Whenever my hopes and dreams have been shattered or my heart has been broken into what seems like a million pieces, it has always been Mom who took the time to help put things back together... with her love.

Chapter 2:
SOMETIMES LOVE
SOMETIMES HURT

Love at First Sight

The first time I saw you
I knew one thing for sure
I was so love sick
And you were my cure

I waited for you
For so very long
Nights of loneliness
Yearning to belong

Into the arms of a lover
Into the heart of a friend
I felt when I held you
My heart start to mend

You've given your love
To this heart once alone
Became my friend/lover
And together we've grown

We will continue to grow
Forever my dear
When it comes to love
Please know I'm sincere

I thank you so much
For all that you do
I've loved you since
The first time I saw you

Three Wishes

I went for a walk
beneath a night's lonely sky.
I was missing my love
when a glimpse caught my eye.
A falling star fell
from heavens, dark above.
So I closed my eyes, made a wish,
for my long lost love.

I saw a fountain pool
while strolling through a mall.
Reached in my pocket,
the fount seemed to call.
I closed my eyes, tossed a coin,
and craved this special wish:
to once again, very soon,
feel her gentle kiss.

Then it was my birthday,
and mother baked a cake.
Before I blew out the candles,
I had this wish to make:
Wherever you are, my love,
wherever that may be,
know how much I love you
and please come back to me.

When My Heart Lacks

When my heart lacks faith
and I struggle day by day
God still blesses me
in His own glorious way

When my heart lacks peace
from the battles deep within
God shelters me with grace
protecting me from sin

When my heart lacks hope
and I want to run and hide
God's care surrounds me
we walk onward side by side

When my heart lacks joy
in my moments of despair
God listens to words
of every tear-soaked prayer

When my heart lacks love
with no light at tunnel's end
God brightens the way
by sending you… my friend

I'll Be There

I know you're going through changes
That may seem too much to bear
But let me reassure you
I love you and I'll be there

To hold you when you need comfort
To listen with much tender care
I'll be the friend you will need
I love you and I'll be there

To cheer you up when you're sad
My life with you I'll share
To warm you when you're cold
I love you and I'll be there

And if for whatever reason
When this life seems unfair
and I can't be there in person
I love you and in spirit I'll be there

If She Had Said 'Don't Go'

I would have grasped her securely in my arms,
whispering soothingly, how much I cared.
Letting her tears flow gently down my shoulder,
as I tenderly announced, "I'm not going anywhere."

I would have kissed her and held her oh so tight,
'til my unwavering grip gave way.
Then looked her deep within her saddened face,
declaring everything would be okay.

I would have been her protector and provider,
gifts of flowers, cards and a simple kiss.
During the times she was not by my side
I would have proved how much she was missed.

I would have cheered her up when she was sad,
treated her like a queen, given her my ring;
every night I would have prayed that in her heart,
I would be her one and only king.

I would have slipped into bed caressing her,
kissing her on the neck, holding her through the night,
waking up staring into her precious green eyes,
making love, at the break of dawn's morning light...

As though I cherished her while she lay sleeping.

26

The Proposal

I know we've had our share of problems
that never seem to go away
but a decision to change for the good
has these words for me to say

I've always loved you no matter what
you were always on my mind
my heart ached painfully
when words you spoke weren't kind

I know our hearts were breaking
I know now things must change
and with a thrill of excitement
I have these plans arranged

For a long time now we've been unhappy
we loved each other in vain
it's going to take time I know
to heal all our pain

From this day forward I promise
to do whatever it takes
to make you happy your life complete
and to cut down on the mistakes

Let's look to the future, forget the past
prove to each other our love
Let's love one another, be best friends again
prove we're a match from heaven above

The words I'm saying are long overdue
I only have myself to blame
I hope you feel my words are sincere
I hope you feel the same

But if you don't I'll understand
just let my heart go free
but if you love me and truly care
then will you marry me?

Upon My Deathbed

If I'm unable to write again,
for my doomed world will soon pass by,
I feel compelled to pen a few lines,
which may fall under your teary eye.

Darling, my love for you is deathless,
for-it shall ever know no end.
Forgive my faults and times I've hurt you,
how thoughtless and foolish I have been.

Yet, you were always there for me,
even if I was the one to blame.
When my last gasp of breath escapes me,
it will be whispering your sweet name.

If the dead can come back to this earth,
and spark unseen around those they love.
You shall know that I will be with you,
bringing love for you to take hold of.

I'll be with you in the brightest day,
and even in the darkest of night.
Amidst your blissful scenes, sad hours,
in spirit, I'll be clutching you tight.

Don't be grief-stricken when I am gone;
allured by your everlasting charm.
I'll always be near, my precious love,
waiting in heaven with open arms.

The Memories I Keep

It was late into the night
And I could not sleep
So I decided to write
On the memories I keep

I miss the way she used to sing
Those old country songs
The way we used to laugh
Made me feel like I belonged

I miss long talks about God
And our crazy families
Sharing hopes and dreams
As well as fantasies

I miss long rides in the car
A yard sale or two
Walking hand and hand
A simple "I love you"

I miss trips to the beach
Long strolls in the park
Watching late-night movies
And whispers in the dark

I miss love before breakfast
And dinners with wine
The warmth of her body
As it lay next to mine

I miss kisses goodbye
Each time we had to part
Warm greetings on return
That came from the heart

But one thing I don't miss
And wish it would end
The sad feeling that arises
When I miss my friend

It was late into the night
And I could not sleep
So I decided to write
On the memories I keep

Mikey

Once in a while, our paths cross with that of someone special who touches our lives. That person changes our lives for the better, many times without knowing it. Often, we do not feel that change immediately. It can take days, weeks, months, or even years before we realize that someone special has impacted our life. Sometimes, we do not get the chance to thank that special someone. When this occurs it's best to continue on in life, touching others in a manner that we too were once touched. By sharing this story, I continue to do so.

I married Sarina, and was raising two girls, Ashley and Rachel, ages six and three. We lived in a small, humble house in the north end of Flint Michigan. My mother and father-in-law lived next door. My brother-in-law lived across the street with his wife and kids, Cody and Brittany. Aunt Sue lived directly behind our home, completing our sense of security, as we were located in one of the roughest parts of the city.

Across the street was a family consisting of three children, a mother, and her crack-dealing boyfriend. I can't remember all their names except for a young boy around the age of five, Mikey. Mikey was deaf, rarely played with any friends, and always seemed to be sad. He was perpetually filthy, his hair was never combed, and he had a constant runny nose. Our family knew very little sign language. *Mother*, *father*, *love*, and *thank you* – was about all we knew. However, a look of confusion appeared on Mikey's dirty face whenever we would try to sign with him. Sarina and I thought this was unusual. Although he was still a young boy, we felt that he should have known some sign language. It didn't take long for us to realize that nobody in his home was concerned enough to teach him. The mother and boyfriend were consumed with dealing drugs, which meant that Mikey's siblings were neglected as well. I immediately started praying for this family.

We had a big yard and it was not unusual to have several kids over playing. One of my favorite things to do was to play baseball with them. I would construct a home plate of old wood or a garbage can lid, walk several paces towards the middle of the yard, drop a pile of softballs (easier to hit than baseballs) at my feet, and proceed to pitch to the little sluggers for batting practice. Both boys and girls received 10 hits each and all the kids had to play the field. This was usually a hilarious event, with kids running, chasing, tripping, and dropping balls all over the yard. Their effort was much appreciated since this required less energy on my part.

On one occasion, I noticed Mikey sitting on his front porch observing attentively while we played. I motioned for him to come over, but he shook his head. I shrugged my shoulders and continued having fun with the kids. A few days passed and once again, we were out in the yard when I noticed Mikey watching us play. This time however, he sat in the center of his yard. I motioned for him to join us, only to be refused again with a sturdy shake of the head. The next time the neighborhood kids were gathered to play baseball, Mikey was sitting even closer, in the ditch. I motioned for him to come over and, surprisingly, he stood up and crossed the dirt road to join the others. I immediately handed him a bat and pointed to the makeshift home plate. With a puzzled look he sluggishly walked to the plate. I realized that he had never held a bat before, so I stood behind him and corrected his grip by uncrossing his hands. I called out to one of the older kids to pitch. Cody won the race to the pitcher's mound. I helped Mikey hold the bat as Cody tossed several balls underhand towards us. I assisted in helping Mikey take the first few cuts and when I felt the time was right, I let him try it solo. I took over the pitching duties, and after a few misses Mikey started to connect, hitting line drives all over the yard. We started losing daylight and had to call it quits, but I'll never forget the smile that lit up Mikey's face as he headed back home.

After that first time playing ball with us, it was not uncommon for me to come home from work and find Mikey in the yard with the kids. He rode the church bus with our kids a couple of times, and several other times he was invited into our home for ice cream. We all did our best to communicate with Mikey by using hand gestures and facial expressions. He was well behaved for the most part, but being a typical little boy, he was sent home a couple of times for roughhousing or annoying the girls. Nonetheless, I grew to love that kid and admired his ability to deal with the many tough difficulties in his life.

Sadly, my marriage succumbed to the trials and tribulations of this world, and Sarina and I broke up. I moved out on my own reluctantly. Sometimes I would inquire about Mikey when I would stop by to visit the kids. I discovered that soon after I had moved away, Mikey's family moved away also. I also heard that his mother's boyfriend had been sexually abusing Mikey's older sister, and that Protective Services took the children away from the mother. I was deeply saddened to hear of this despicable abuse but I had faith that Mikey's circumstances would improve as a result of the state's intervention.

As the years passed, I sometimes thought about Mikey and wondered what had happened to him. One day, I sat down to read the newspaper and saw a picture of two adults standing with a boy. After further examination, I realized that the boy was Mikey. The article explained that the pair would be the first deaf, married couple to adopt a deaf child. To my surprise, it was the first such case in the state of Michigan. I was moved to tears of joy because it seemed Mikey had finally found a good home. I remember thinking that he would certainly learn some sign language now!

It's been many years since our paths crossed but I still do think about Mikey on occasion. It's been several years since the article was published in *The Flint Journal* and even longer since he played ball in my yard, yet in only a short time he touched my family and me in a remarkable way. He helped me teach my children that despite being deaf, he was still a person, in need of love and attention, and should be treated like all people, with kindness and respect. I doubt our paths will ever cross again but I am a much kinder, gentler, understanding person, having known Mikey. I hope life has been good to him and he has continued to touch people with his kind, courageous spirit.

Chapter 3:
LOVER OF MY SOUL

A Decision to Change

A change came upon me one glorious day.
It lifted me up, helped change my ways.
It took this troubled heart and filled it with love.
No doubt in my mind it was the Lord from heaven above.
I opened my heart and let Him come in.
He changed my life, washed away my sins.
He touched me in a way I can't explain.
He helped comfort my heart, helped heal the pain.
He gave me the message "Come walk with me",
and "You shall receive eternal life, you shall be set free."
Hearing this message I could not turn away.
And with this change, I'm happy to say,
the choice was mine; at first, I admit I was afraid.
But I chose to serve the Lord – the best decision I ever made.

My Best Friend

I want you to meet my best friend.
I've known Him for many a year
and His love for me knows no end.
With strength like that whom shall I fear?

He's been with me through success,
and in times I was a failure.
Whatever problem comes my way,
He is by my side with a cure.

He accepts me the way I am.
That very acceptance makes me,
in spite of all of my faults,
want to be all I can be.

He laughs with me over mistakes
and weeps with me when I am sad.
He's been faithful throughout my life,
the best friend a man ever had.

His love for me has no limits.
He's loyal when others turn away.
He listens to each of my hurts
and to whatever else I say.

One day I'll see Him face to face,
when life on earth for me must end.
I hope then that it's said of me,
"Jesus Christ was his best friend."

Supreme Mercy and Grace

We have all betrayed the Lord
In our lives at various times
But the secret is to admit our sin
When the convicting Spirit shines

So seek God's forgiveness
When we repent, He forgives
No matter how great the sin
Still in our hearts He lives

In fact, nothing in all creation
That is so horrible, big or small
Can separate us from God's,
Unconditional love for us all

No need to despair for our lives
Stop all lingering guilt or shame
Ask God for His forgiving mercy
In Jesus' precious name

So remember to confess our sins
Everyday while we pray
Jesus knows our every weakness
And He still loves us anyway

What am I to Do?

My sweet Jesus, I call out to you.
Oh, sweet Jesus, what am I to do?

If ever I needed you, now is the time.
Search my heart, I'm sure you will find
pain and hurt, like never before.
With each passing day I need you more.
Help me to do that which is right
so others may see in me your perfect light.
Please forgive me for the mistakes I've made.
At the foot of the cross my sins I've laid.
Thank you for dying on the cross for me
and giving me new life for eternity.
For this, my life will never be the same.
May I bring honor and glory, to your sweet name.

My sweet Jesus, I've called out to you!
Oh, sweet Jesus, what am I to do?

My Victory

My joy he stole, that nasty foe,
'till Jesus heard my plea
From the hole that brought me low
A life of misery

My heart, once coal, was washed white as snow
I hope you will agree
Sin took its toll but now I glow
for all the world to see

To save my soul so I could grow
to what I need to be
He played the role and had to show
His perfect love for me

Now that I'm whole may others know
just how I was set free
Upon a knoll His blood did flow
for my victory

Mourning Glory

My room so cold and lonely,
teardrops flood my eyes.
The rain outside descending
from dark and stormy skies.

I sit alone and ponder
on good times that used to be,
but the only days I have now,
fill up with misery.

I try accepting what'ss happened
make plans for coming years,
but every passing moment
only brings new tears.

I sit here by my window
with rain slowly falling,
as I close mourning eyes
I realize someone's calling.

I wipe the hurt from my face,
and bow my head to pray.
At last I turn to the Son,
who dries my tears away!

The Plan

Help me, Jesus, to understand.
What is your will, your plan?
Is there hope for a wretch like me?
Of a life of sin, I'm guilty.

Yes, my child, you need not fear,
because you called I am near.
Even during the times you fall,
I'll pick you up when you call.

I possess no gifts or talents.
That doesn't matter, does it?
Can you save me from my past,
show me love that will last?

Confess your sins everyday.
Read your Bible and always pray.
I will love you for who you are,
I'm forever near, never far.

Thank you for dying on the cross
and saving me when I was lost.
I believe in you and I'm prepared,
but oh, how my life needs repair.

Not just faith … you need trust.
Surrender to me, it's a must.
I'll change your world, renew your heart,
and give your life a fresh new start.

Thank you, Jesus, for all you do.
Help me to better serve you.
Bring you honor, with little shame.
Bring much glory to your name.

Now you know what is my will.
It won't be easy, but still,
commit to me to understand,
for all along that was my plan.

My Memories of Ernie Harwell

Detroit Tigers Radio Commentator Ernie Harwell
(January 25, 1918–May 4, 2010)

As I look back upon my life, there are few people I could listen to for several hours without objection, my Pastor, Walter Cronkite, Paul Harvey, and Ernie Harwell. Of the four names mentioned, it was Ernie, who evoked the most emotion and unforgettable memories that I will forever cherish.

Ron LeFlore swiping bases, Tram and Sweet Lou turning two, Morris pitching another gem, and Big Cecil smashing another *long-gone* home run, are only a few of the many pictures that are embedded in my mind, from the countless days and nights of listening to Ernie's play-by-play on the radio. Throughout the years of my youth and well into my adult life, nobody helped shape me into the devoted Detroit Tigers fan I am today, like Ernie Harwell.

When my mom thought I was in my bedroom doing my homework or sleeping comfy in my bed, I was secretly listening to Ernie on my little transistor radio. I remember the sudden fear I often felt, after waking up in the morning and realizing that Ernie's familiar voice, once again, had gently put me to sleep with the radio still on. Explaining to my mother why I needed yet another 9V battery was never an easy task. (I apologize to Duracell for Mom not believing that they had the longest-running battery on the market. In her defense, I must confess: it was Ernie's fault!)

The 1984 Tigers are my favorite sport memory. Roaring off to a 35-5 start, my beloved Tigers ran away with the pennant, eventually winning the World Series in five games over the San Diego Padres. I never complained if the Tigers were not on T.V, for I knew I could always catch the game on WJR AM 760 with Ernie. Although I admit that I watched most games and all of the post-season on T.V, I also rushed to turn on the radio after those same games to catch the recap and to share in the sincere enthusiasm and pure enjoyment with the biggest Tigers fan I knew.

I never met Ernie but I felt that I knew him personally. He was there for many pick-up games, summer cookouts, trips to the beach and even family vacations. He was and always will be part of my family. If there is baseball in heaven, without a doubt, it is Ernie who will be doing the broadcasting. I know I speak for thousands of fans that all feel the same across our great state – Ernie was truly a Michigan icon.

The impeccable character that Ernie always demonstrated, even if the Tigers were struggling to win games, is what I admired most. In a world where too often people turn their backs on each other because of mistakes and unfulfilled personal expectations, Ernie always remained faithful.

Whether or not the Tigers are fighting to win the pennant or clawing out from the cellar, I will follow Ernie's example and cheer, "Go Tigers

Chapter 4:
STORY TIME WITH UNCLE DAVID

Mean Halloween

Concerned, I said "yes"
and hung up the phone.
This Halloween night
I would be alone.

I just received word
at home I must stay.
A scary monster
was headed my way.

It wanted the kids.
This, my greatest fear,
I warned the children,
as evil grew near.

They had such courage
as they hugged me tight.
One had to remind me,
"Turn on the porch light!"

I flipped on the switch
as I looked outside.
The creature was coming;
there was no time to hide.

The house began to shake
as it approached the door.
I wasn't ready
for what was in store.

The strangest thing
my eyes ever saw,
was dressed like a clown,
my ex-mother-in-law!

"Let's go trick-or-treating!"
she said with a smile.
"Start passing out candy,
we'll be back in a while."

Facebook Love

It must have been your profile pic
That first attracted me to you
And I knew it must have been fate
As I read your info through

I giggled like a sweet little girl
When you accepted my friend request
I cherished every picture posted
I like the one on the boat the best

My smitten heart was relieved
When I saw you weren't underage
And my love grew like my friends list
With each hour on your page

I never missed your status update
Or each posted music video
I even started playing Farmville
So I could help your farm grow

I blushed with each comment
You left beneath my notes
And you really made my day
When you started to "like" my quotes

We shared the same interests
Like reading, writing and Family Guy
And in times you were not online
I wanted to log off and cry

I knew I had found my true love
And I was ready to commit
So I asked you to be my girl
Your no I will soon not forget

Now messages go unanswered
There are no replies to my chat
I gaze at the computer screen
Eating Cheetos and getting fat

So I've decided to move on
Although my heart remains sore
By accepting this sad fact
You don't "poke" me anymore

Mountain Joe

Once upon a different time, many years ago,
lived a ballplayer, who was called Mountain Joe.
Baseball was his passion and he held a special dream –
to play the game he loved, for a major league team.

He possessed broad shoulders, stood 6-foot 4,
and could smack homeruns that would soar.
He pitched fiercely with a rocket for an arm,
and could run down rabbits, back on the farm.

Men admired him, women loved his good looks,
kids often begged him, to autograph their books.
A hero to many and the toast of the town,
treated like a cherished king, without the crown.

Playing in the city league, he stood above the rest,
and everyone agreed, "Mountain Joe was the best!"
Whether he was pitching or standing at the plate,
opposing players trembled; Joe controlled their fate.

He led the Giants to the championship game,
against cross-town rivals – the Eagles was their name.
As the game approached, word spread all about,
for sitting in the stands that day was a major league scout!

Stores closed early, the stadium filled fast,
thousands came to watch the game, the seasons last.
The aroma of popcorn and hot dogs filled the air,
and rumor had it all the townsfolk were there.

The anthem was sung, Joe strolled to the mound,
and the ballpark thundered with a deafening sound.
Applause erupted and hearts filled with pride,
as Mountain Joe promptly, struck out the side.

Bell and Gus flew out before Joe's turn to bat;
Joe smashed a double to right and tipped his hat.
There he stayed, unable to advance.
Brown struck out, so back to the mound Joe pranced.

Both teams battled on this unforgettable day.
The Eagles hung tough; they had come to play.
Joe had 14 strikeouts and batted 4 for 4,
but in the bottom of the ninth, still no score.

Knowing only one run was all they needed,
Joe walked to the plate, as the children pleaded,
"You can do it, Mountain Joe, don't be outdone,
show those Eagles a long homerun!"

Joe tightened his grip and spit out his chaw,
and glared at the pitcher with a stiffened jaw.
Determined not to fail or to be outclassed,
Joe swung at the ball and there was a blast.

Where the ball landed nobody knows,
all agreed it was a powerful blow.
The umpire spoke up, ending the suspense,
and announced to the crowd, "Over the fence!"
With the ump's declaration Joe circled the bases.
Except for the Eagles, elation was on all faces.
Joe was mobbed at home plate, fans cheered his name,
and that is the story how Mountain Joe won the game.

After the game, the scout found Mountain Joe
and admitted to him, "You are the best I know!"
"It was a treat to watch you, but I won't be back.
It's a darn shame, kid, that you were born black."

The Hustle

There once was a man
who loved to play pool.
They called him "Ritter."
He thought he was cool.

He would enter tournaments
all over the town.
Walking into any bar
all the people would frown.

Nobody could beat him,
even on his worst night.
He got under people's skin,
his attitude wasn't right.

He laughed, bragged and cussed,
it got worse with each drink.
After sinking the 8-ball
he would turn with a wink.

Then came a challenge
from a little old lady.
"I'm not afraid of you!"
she said standing 5' 3

Not one to back down,
Ritter agreed to play.
Being the jerk he was,
he asked her, "Do you wanna pray?"

"I need not pray, you turd,
for I'm gonna kick your ass.
To make things interesting
let's play for cash!"

With a smirk on his face,
he agreed to play for a stake.
Thinking it was easy money
Ritter offered her the break.

The bar came to a stand still,
the patrons gathered around.
They were eager to watch.
You could not hear a sound.

Chalking her bar stick,
she announced to the crowd.
"8-ball in the side pocket
you all will be proud."

Leaning over the table,
she broke the balls.
The 8-ball found the side pocket.
Game over, she made her call.

She walked up to Ritter
to collect her money.
"Thanks for the game,
you're not so hot now, honey."

In memory of Sally Hissong (Northgate bar) 4/17/30- 10/20/09

The Kind Man

Joe sat in his gloomy, dark cell,
staring at the black walls of stone,
when a recurring thought of her
reminded him he was alone.
Because she no longer loved him
Joe felt like he had lost all hope.
He snatched a dirty sheet off his bunk,
to carefully fashion a rope.

But before taking such drastic measures,
Joe needed to know for sure.
Perhaps she cared enough to write,
and then maybe his heart could endure.
So he waited day after day,
as the long months slowly passed by.
At the end of each wretched night
Joe had found more reasons to die,
'cause not only did she not write,
his friends were also long gone.
When the mail passed by his cell
Joe had not a letter, not one.

Feeling forgotten and all alone,
Joe no longer wanted to wait.
A calendar hung on the wall;
he decided to choose a date.
It was the month of December.
Christmas day was a week away.
Joe thought, "I'll help them remember",
and he circled the 25th day.

With the holiday forthcoming,
never once did Joe have a doubt.
The best time to fulfill his wish
was 10 p.m. after lights out.
Joe went about his business,
as the chosen day arrived.
Nobody had the slightest clue
that soon he would not be alive.

Joe walked into the dining hall
and then settled down to eat his chow.
Suddenly he heard a voice say,
"You can go to heaven, know how?"
Joe looked up from his half-eaten meal,
and sitting straight across from him
was a kind man who spoke the words;
once again he repeated them.
"You can go to heaven, know how?"
he remarked with a peaceful smile.
"If you're interested at all,
church starts in a little while."
Joe nodded with a solemn frown,
knowing all the bad he'd done.
Then asked, "Will you be at the service?"
The man said, "I never miss one!"
The kind man rose up and added,
"Make sure that you're not late,
they're having a birthday party,
and the celebration starts at eight."

Joe rushed back to his dreary cell,
stretched out upon the harsh bed,
and could not stop thinking about
everything the kind man had said.
It was unusual, he thought,
"I've never seen the man before,"
but still he decided he'd go,
it was an invite he could not ignore.

At 8 p.m. Joe strolled into church
and started to look around
for the friend he'd met earlier,
yet he was nowhere to be found.
Disappointment set in again
because the kind man was not there.
A disheartened Joe marched to the back,
found refuge in an empty chair.

Frustrated, he wanted to leave
before the service was to start,
but the music started playing
to the depths of Joe's sullen heart.
As the sweet melody faded,
a gent stood up, called Preacher Dave,
who began telling the story
of a brave baby, born to save.
When this precious child matured
he healed the sick, gave sight to the blind,
and courageously died on the cross
for the sins of all of mankind.
All can come to Him in prayer
for the forgiveness of all sin.
If they would open up their hearts
a loving Savior would come in.

The most wonderful thing Joe heard,
about learning how to be set free.
One day he could go to heaven,
and live for all eternity!

The story was so interesting,
enthralling Joe's full attention.
When Preacher Dave finished preaching
he gave out an invitation.

Gradually, Joe worked up the courage,
although he was afraid,
stepped forward to accept Jesus,
the wisest choice he ever made.

After the service was over
an inmate handed Dave a gift
and announced, "Merry Christmas, Preacher,
I hope it gives your heart a lift!"
It was a portrait of Jesus that
the inmate proudly painted.
When the pleased preacher held it up
a shocked Joe nearly fainted.
For the image stroked on canvas,
in the inmate's own style,
was no other than Joe's Kind Man,
wearing an ever-peaceful smile!

Lonesome Christmas

I am alone on Christmas day
Without a single friend
No Christmas cheer to give away
Nor Christmas cards to send

No table with a Christmas spread
No star above a tree
No fat man with a suit of red
Will stop to visit me

No kisses under the mistletoe
No bells for me to ring
No present with a shiny bow
No Christmas songs to sing

No visits from my family
No home to call my own
One more Christmas memory
One more day alone

A Lesson Learned

Miss Gregg was a concerned teacher
who proudly taught elementary.
She had a problem student
and his name was Little Johnny.

Little Johnny liked to tell fibs
and everyone was sick of them.
So Miss Gregg had a bright idea:
she'd tell her own tall tale to him.

Then perhaps Johnny would realize
just how silly it was to lie,
and maybe he'd stop doing it.
She thought, "It's worth a try."

Approaching Little Johnny,
she said, "Guess what happened to me?
I was hiking through the forest,
enjoying all the scenery.
As I walked down a rustic trail
that followed along a wide stream,
I noticed standing on his hind legs
a grizzly that caused me to scream!

This beast was about to attack
when a small dog charged from the woods
and knocked down that angry ol' bear
where that big, ugly brute once stood.

They rolled and tussled in a brawl,
'til one of them had wounds that bled.
The wiener dog was left standing,
while that grizzly bear lay dead.

Then that dog clutched that big ol' bear
and dragged the beaten foe away.
While I safely walked onward,
enjoying this most bizarre day.

Now what do you think of that Johnny?"
His thoughts appeared lost in a fog,
until he grinned from ear to ear
and announced, "Hey, that was my dog!"

Springtime Cheer

Of all the seasons in the year
Springs the one that gives me cheer

For longer days and a brighter sun
That melts the snow when winters done
A good riddance to winter strife
A pleasant welcome for new life

For maple syrup on my plate
Croaking frogs court a mate
Wild flowers erupt in bloom
Sweeping the garage with a broom

For the birds safe return
Cleaning the boat stem to stern
Firing up the barbecue grill
As mother earth sprouts daffodils

For the child with bat and ball
Who runs the bases and does not fall
All teams begin in first place
With visions of a pennant race

For the bunnies who hop along
Beneath the robins who sing their song
High atop a cherry tree
Where blossoms burst in majesty

Of all the seasons in the year
Springs the one that gives me cheer

The Sultan of Swat

Teachers are not given enough recognition for the hard work that they do in helping develop students into young adults. One such teacher was Mr. Jacques. I remember the ill feeling I had when I first learned that I would be one of his students entering the fourth grade. Mr. Jacques was a notorious teacher around Briggs Elementary School for giving students swats. Rumor had it he was a very mean teacher and the worst one to have in the whole school. He was a burly looking fellow who resembled Babe Ruth, except Mr. Jacques sported a mustache. He owned a paddle made of wood, the size of my mother's frying pan, which would have made Babe Ruth proud. It also had holes drilled into it for better sting. He proudly displayed the paddle on the wall next to the chalkboard in front of the class and Mr. Jacques achieved many hits with this paddle thanks to my backside. Although he was strict, when need be, he was also fair. I now feel that he was a very good teacher who taught me many things. He happened to teach both the fourth grade as well as the fifth grade in the same classroom, and as fate would have it, I also had him for a teacher in the that grade. It was during those two years that I learned and accomplished a lot.

During one of those years, Mr. Jacques held a contest for the student who could read the most books. We had to give him a written book report to help prove that we read the book. He displayed every student's name on a poster board that was tacked up on the bulletin board. Each time a classmate read a book and submitted a report, Mr. Jacques would put a gold, shiny star sticker next to the student's name. By the end of the year my name had the most stars and Mr. Jacques rewarded me with my very first thesaurus. Prior to receiving it, I never knew what a thesaurus was. I still use it daily because of my love for writing.

It was during this time that I fell in love with books. My favorites were biographies. I read books about Abraham Lincoln, Anne Oakley, Kit Carson, Daniel Webster, Davy Crockett, and many more. My favorite book was about Jim Thorpe, who is considered one of the greatest athletes of all time. It was this book that helped introduce me to sports. I began playing elementary football and basketball during the fourth grade. To this day, I am still a big fan of a variety of sports.

Every year our class would have a spelling bee. Mr. Jacques would line the whole class in front of the room along the chalkboard. When a classmate would misspell a word, they would have to go back to their seat. One year after several rounds, I was the last boy standing next to another classmate, Tonya, who was the last girl. Tonya missed a word and Mr. Jacques gave me the word "arithmetic." One of my best friends, Mike, started laughing out loud. He knew that my mother had just recently taught me how to spell that word by taking the first letter of each word from the sentence, "A red Indian thought he may eat tomatoes in church." As I was spelling this word verbally, I was slowly repeating the sentence in my mind and reciting the first letter of each word. After spelling the word correctly I was declared the winner. I was able to represent my school in the district to compete against other students from other area schools. I'm sorry to admit that I didn't perform very well. I was knocked out of the competition in the first round on the word "ability." Despite my poor showing in the district spelling bee, it was still an honor to represent my school and a proud accomplishment.

It was also during the fourth and fifth grades that I learned the game of chess. Mr. Jacques taught everyone in the class how to play. After several weeks of practicing, Mr. Jacques held a single game elimination chess tournament. After winning several matches, I made it to the championship, where I lost to a boy named Thomas. Because of Mr. Jacques taking the time to teach his students the game, I went on to play on the high school chess team and still enjoy chess today.

I often wonder what happened to Mr. Jacques. Briggs Elementary is no longer open. Sadly, it was torn down several years ago. It is amazing how a teacher can have such an impact on one student's life. Today my love for sports, the game of chess, reading, and writing, can all be attributed to the two years I had Mr. Jacques for a teacher. Despite all the swats I received, which I'm sure I deserved, I feel that Mr. Jacques was the best teacher I ever had. I regret that I never told him, "Thank you, for all that you taught me," and I wish now that there was some way I could. I owe him a debt of gratitude for all he taught me while I was a boy, and he deserves a great deal of recognition for helping to shape me into the man that I am today.

Printed in Great Britain
by Amazon

37388085R00036